MW01675611

What People Are Saying About *In Pursuit of Leadership*

There are perhaps more books written on the topic of leadership than any other on the market. Countless individuals from all walks of life have examined leadership from every conceivable angle, leaving precious little fruit to be plucked from the tree. So, it would seem…

William Tyler King sets out in his book, *In Pursuit of Leadership*, with one bold agenda in mind—to assist readers in discovering and developing the hidden leader that exists within every person. King does a masterful job of steering clear of a theoretical discussion and presents us with clear, concise, and actionable principles on leadership that anyone can apply. His basic premise is refreshingly simple. He believes that leadership is a blend of art and science, and the final product improves over time as a result of four principle ingredients that he spells out in the book.

What I find most fascinating about the book is the clear roadmap King outlines and the Leadership Formula he identifies to assist readers in locating the leader within.

By the time the reader puts this book down, I am convinced that he or she will conclude as I have that *In Pursuit of Leadership* has achieved every benchmark that William Tyler King set out to accomplish.

—**Gary N. Sparkman**, author of *Dare to Discover Yourself*

Brilliantly simple and inspiring! From character to commitment, *In Pursuit of Leadership* shines a bright light on the path to trusted leadership!

—**David Horsager**, speaker, consultant,
author of the national bestseller, *The Trust Edge*

In his book, *In Pursuit of Leadership*, King offers a perspective on leadership that is both useful and needed. In contrast to some of the more hero-worshiping books on leadership, King offers a valuable framework for those in leadership's more formative stages. His emphasis on the importance of individual character traits is refreshing compared to the more value-free approaches advocated in some spheres. King suggests that emerging leaders can benefit by observing effective leaders and drawing useable practices and philosophies from these observations. King wisely counsels the emerging leader to both prepare, by nurturing their own leadership styles, and to employ patience and understanding in our competitive and challenging corporate world. *In Pursuit of Leadership* is well worth reading.

—**Frederick M. Zimmerman**, Ph.D., Emeritus Professor,
University of St. Thomas, author of *The Turnaround Experience: Real World Lessons in Revitalizing Corporations*,
member of the boards of directors of several corporations

In Pursuit of Leadership demonstrates that great leadership is a journey of learning and growth. A must read for everyone wanting to grow their leadership skills.

—**Rich Wagner**, Ph.D.,
President, Dunwoody College of Technology

When I coached Tyler King at Army, he always came prepared to play. It's no wonder that his leadership focus is on preparation and commitment. Before the 1960 Winter Olympics in Squaw Valley, I was told many times that we could never beat the Russians in hockey. As everyone knows, we did it! A few months after we won gold and the U.S. team was preparing for the 1960 Summer Olympics in Rome, I was asked to disclose our hockey team's secret to success. I wrote down these five points: Plan better, Conserve our best players, Pick our team properly, Get in top shape, and Go first class. These five points are all about preparation: start with the right plan with the right players who are in the right condition first and then go for gold. Tyler's book is a must-read for coaches and leaders looking for an edge on the competition.

—**Jack Riley**, Head Coach, West Point Hockey Team, 1950–1986, Gold Medal, 1960 Squaw Valley Winter Olympics

King does an excellent job of using his own military and sports experiences to bring home some very relevant concepts in leadership. He further illustrates his common sense and relatable approach to leadership with some of the all-time great leaders in military and sports. I've already started using the exercises and next steps provided at the end of each chapter. I have no doubt I'll be a more effective leader before the year is done, thanks to *In Pursuit of Leadership*!

—**Karen White**, Executive Director, 360° Manufacturing and Applied Engineering Center of Excellence, Bemidji State University

I am pleased to see a book on leadership coming from William Tyler King. His background and experience has placed him in a position to influence today's emerging leaders. In the tech industry, where I have worked since graduating from Stanford University in 1985, we stress words like "innovation," but in the end, it is excellent leadership that makes the narrow difference between failure and success. Mr. King's insights remind us that anything of value, and certainly something as important as learning to be a true leader, takes commitment and effort.

I find Mr. King's equations to be spot-on. They are new and simple ways to think about difficult-to-define concepts such as "character" and "winning." None of these equations would be possible without the fundamental principle that you must lead by example. I know few people who rival Mr. William Tyler King in this regard.

—**Sam Neff**, Senior Vice President Technology, Pearson English

In Pursuit of Leadership is a practical guide for individuals who long for the opportunity to lead, yet feel they weren't born leaders. King reaches back to the practice of apprenticeship to articulate the key components of leadership. Based on his strong educational background at West Point, his practical experience as a young Army officer, and his tenure as a professor at the University of Minnesota, King brings a unique perspective to the leadership development discussion. I am excited to see how *In Pursuit of Leadership* will impact current and future generations of leaders!

—**Larry Smith**, United States Military Academy at West Point, Class of 1984, President, Tokyo Electron America, Inc.

Educating students in the qualities of leadership requires extensive past experiences, the ability to be introspective, and the vision to look forward and create the foundation needed to develop our future leaders. Through his education at West Point, his participation in Division I athletics, and his Manufacturing in a Global Economy courses at the University of Minnesota, King has demonstrated the passion and plea for enhanced leadership education. This book is an excellent exposé of what is required to be a committed, recognized leader in today's society. I would highly recommend his book as a part of your leadership reading armamentarium.

—**M. Mark Melin**, M.D., F.A.C.S., Park Nicollet Heart and Vascular Center, Clinical Associate Professor, University of Minnesota, Department of Surgery

William Tyler King couples his years of leadership experience with a knack for distilling ideas and concepts to create one of the most useful books I have ever read. I could have put this book to good use three decades ago before I started my first rite of passage into a leadership role. *In Pursuit of Leadership* is packed with practical advice and real-life examples that illuminate the cornerstones of good leadership: character, study, preparation, and commitment. Read this book and you'll see your leadership journey in a whole new light. I highly recommend this book for anyone seeking to emerge as a leader.

—**Erick Ajax**, Co-Owner of EJ Ajax Metal Forming Solutions

In Pursuit of Leadership outlines a clear and simple method to becoming a values-driven leader of substance, authenticity, and resiliency. King's book is a unique and excellent guide for anyone's leadership journey.

—**Tom Wiese**, WieseLaw Contract Studio
and Co-Founder of Studio/E

Tyler King hits the mark when he says that leadership is both art and science. At its essence, leadership is anchored in a person's character. Out of many strong points made in his book, Tyler highlights the importance of being a student of leadership. Good leaders don't just lead; they lead by emulating what they admire in others and also drawing out the best in each person.

—**Nate Garvis**, Author of Naked Civics, Co-Founder of Studio/E

Our culture holds a jaded view of leadership. That is why I think *In Pursuit of Leadership* is spot on! We all have leadership skills we can hone and put into action. Our nation seems to be on the status-quo train to nowhere. I'm eager to see King's book help frame this important discussion on leadership. For 30 years, I've known King as a quiet, confident, example-setting leader who will wake up the leader in you!

—**M. Brian Cotter**, CEO of IT services company
with over 900 employees, West Point hockey team 1979–1983

Great leaders are committed to the success of their team. King's book took me through the process of apprenticeship and character building used by true leaders. I was quite surprised to learn of the circumstances of these heroes! King shows us that great leadership starts with self-assessment and an unselfish commitment to help others succeed. His leadership equations lay the groundwork for understanding the most important tool on the belt—me!

—**Brian K. Bolstad**, Manufacturing Team Supervisor

In Pursuit *of* Leadership

A Real Guide for Emerging Leaders

WILLIAM TYLER KING

TCLA
Twin Cities Leadership Academy

In Pursuit of Leadership
A Real Guide for Emerging Leaders
by Tyler King

Published by:
TCLA
Twin Cities Leadership Academy
Twin Cities Leadership Academy
3415 Sycamore Lane N., Plymouth, MN 55441
www.TwinCitiesLeadershipAcademy.com

www.InPursuitofLeadership.com

© 2014 by William Tyler King. All rights reserved. Printed and Bound in the United States of America. No part of this book may be reproduced or transmitted in any form or by any means, electronic or mechanical, including photocopying, recording, or by an information storage and retrieval system—except by a reviewer who may quote brief passages in a review to be printed in a magazine, newspaper, or on the Web—without permission in writing from the author. For information, please contact King@InPursuitofLeadership.com

Although the author and publisher have made every effort to ensure the accuracy and completeness of information contained in this book, we assume no responsibility for errors, inaccuracies, omissions, or any inconsistency herein. Any slights of people, places, or organizations are unintentional.

Unattributed quotations are by Tyler King

Cover and interior design by Purpose Design

ISBN 978-0-9897481-1-7

1st edition

1. Business. 2. Leadership.

ATTENTION CORPORATIONS, UNIVERSITIES, COLLEGES AND PROFESSIONAL ORGANIZATIONS: Quantity discounts are available on bulk purchases of this book. Special books or book excerpts can also be created to fit special needs. For information, please contact King@InPursuitofLeadership.com

Dedication

For my mother who taught me
eternal optimism,

and

in memory of my father,
the finest man I've ever known.

SOME SAY LEADERSHIP BOOKS are a dime a dozen. While that may be true, I find most of them to be either too tedious or too vague. They either leave me with a list too long to possibly implement or a model too broad for me to find the one kernel of practical wisdom.

This book is my attempt to provide leaders with the right blend of detail and big picture. It is dedicated to the countless supervisors, factory foremen, team leads, coaches, and community leaders on the front lines, who are down in the trenches every day faced with leadership challenges. This book's sole purpose is to help prepare new and emerging leaders for one of the most important journeys of their lives—their leadership journey. It is my hope that you will use it to guide you on your daily pursuit to be the best leader you can be!

—Tyler King

CONTENTS

ACKNOWLEDGEMENTS

I WANT TO GIVE A SINCERE THANK YOU to the many colleagues who provided feedback on my book and gave me their endorsement. I have great respect for your individual leadership pursuits as well as your willingness to guide emerging leaders. Thanks for your contribution, Erick Ajax, Brian K. Bolstad, M. Brian Cotter, Nate Garvis, David Horsager, Dr. Mark Melin, Sam Neff, Jack Riley, Larry Smith, Gary N. Sparkman, Damian Topousis, Rich Wagner, Karen White, Tom Wiese, and Frederick M. Zimmerman. Thank you to my editor, Heidi Sheard, for your attention to detail. You helped me stay true to my vision for this project. And likewise, thank you to my designer, Heidi Koopman, of Purpose Design, for her excellent work on the cover and interior design.

To the hundreds of students who have been through my classes at the University of Minnesota, thank you for helping me understand your generation and the importance for us to strip away the redundant jargon that plagues most leadership books. For you, the emerging leaders of today, I wrote *In Pursuit of Leadership*.

FOREWORD

AFTER READING *In Pursuit of Leadership: A Real Guide for Emerging Leaders*, I've been able to relate Tyler's career experience and accomplishments with the person I've known for forty years. I'd like to share with you a little bit about William Tyler King so that you have a better perspective of why he's the perfect authority to write a book on leadership.

Qualities important to a leader are bravery and courage. Tyler and I attended a fairly rough public junior high school in a suburb of St. Paul, Minnesota. Picture this: a rough public school has a school-wide talent show and shy, 15 year-old Tyler King steps out to perform a tap dancing routine to Sweet Georgia Brown that would have made Fred Astaire smile! He didn't worry about what the tough guys thought; he took lessons, practiced diligently, and then showed us what he could do. Tyler displayed bravery and courage to the nth degree that day! His hard work and excellence gained respect, and every year thereafter, we looked forward to watching Tyler in the talent show.

Another incredibly important quality of good leaders is teamwork. In high school, Tyler was the Captain and All-State Quarterback on our football team, All-Conference Winger on our hockey team, and Captain and All-State Shortstop on our baseball team. Even with all this talent and recognition, Tyler was better known as the ultimate team player. His strengths weren't so much his ability to score runs and goals or to rush the football down the field, but his humble approach of making each individual teammate a better player. Somehow Tyler always had a unique ability to make even the weakest players feel like they were contributing to the overall success of the team.

When I heard that Tyler was turning down a number of opportunities to play any one of his three sports at a major university in order to attend the United States Military Academy at West Point, it struck me that William Tyler King was destined to be a leader. The training that West Point gave him to be an officer, to lead men and women into the field of battle, and to guide and teach them, was the perfect path for Tyler. To add to his bravery, courage, and teamwork, Tyler developed discipline and loyalty.

I know Tyler has written this book with his own unique perspective and style. I am also confident that as you read this book and thoughtfully relate the lessons Tyler has shared, you will undoubtedly become a better leader yourself. As you enjoy this book, I encourage you to think about others who could benefit from this carefully written guide for emerging leaders.

—**Damian Topousis,** Founder, The Dojo Group

The journey
is better
than the inn.

—Cervantes

INTRODUCTION

EARLIER IN MY CAREER, I was not particularly extroverted, nor did I display excess amounts of social maturity. In fact, I lacked self-confidence and often struggled with insecurity. I went from high school to the United States Military Academy at West Point where I received a B.S. in Engineering. Even after my rigorous training at West Point, I had no tangible military leadership experience and did not fully appreciate the rewards of soldiering. It was only after I was thrust into my first leadership position as a Field Artillery Officer and subsequent leadership positions both in the Army and in my civilian career that real leadership development began. It was through these many experiences that I gained the confidence to lead. More importantly, I found the excitement that leadership generates, and the professional satisfaction that comes from knowing the job was done well—not by me, but by my team who I had the privilege and responsibility of guiding and influencing.

Leadership is not some inevitable lot in life. My personal leadership journey has taught me that effective leadership comes through a complex learning process, limited and affected by our individual experiences. Leadership is a dynamic and constructive process that develops not in a day, but every single day. Good leadership requires action—the right action. As Max De Pree stated, "Leadership is the right actions taken in the context of clear and well-considered thinking."

Leadership develops not in a day, but every single day.

There is nothing particularly fancy that I can teach you about leadership—nothing that requires special gifts, traits, or privileges. Rather, leadership requires dedication to three principles outlined in this book: Character Matters; Leadership Takes Time; and Preparation Needs Commitment. From this theoretical foundation, *In Pursuit of Leadership* examines the premise that leadership is a combination of art and science developed and improved over years of experience, reflection, intervention, and self-development. One's experience as a follower is an invaluable contribution to his or her pursuit of leadership.

Experience as a follower is invaluable to the pursuit of leadership.

In the end, perhaps the most important question about leadership is whether to pursue it at all. Ultimately, it's up to each of us to realize that strong leadership is an outcome of life-long preparation and commitment—a journey of self-development. The simple purpose of *In Pursuit of Leadership* is to help us find and develop that leader within us.

❧

FOR MORE THAN 20 YEARS, I've worked with many young men and women interested in positions requiring direct leadership responsibility. I always ask them, "What's the most important part of the job?" I get many different answers, but very few answer, "Leadership." This tells me that leadership needs to find its way back to the front lines. As the founder of the Twin Cities Leadership Academy, it is my intention to arm new leaders with key leadership principles that, when used with thoughtful introspection, unlock the leader within them so they can become the leader they want to be.

This book is divided into three chapters. Chapter one answers the questions What is character? and Why is character important in effective leadership? It also introduces a strategy to improve your Character Equation. Chapter two confirms the effectiveness of apprenticeships in leadership development by studying the long leadership journeys of two great American heroes, Robert E. Lee and Dwight D. Eisenhower. It also defines the Leadership Formula and provides a strategy to improve it. Chapter three introduces the idea that preparation requires commitment and commitment takes extraordinary effort. The leader's ability to influence their team's discretionary effort is the heart of leadership and defines the leader's effectiveness.

It is generally believed that leadership is 20% observation, 20% learned from books, and 60% trial and error. Like the apprenticeship programs developed for artisan trades, the bulk of learning is experienced on the job; however, the importance of education in leadership cannot be underestimated. The word education comes from the Latin 'ex' meaning "out," and 'duco' meaning "I lead." Essentially, education is a leading out of that which is already inside us. In their book, *The Leadership Challenge*, James Kouzes and Barry Posner warn against developmental processes that are intrusive. It should never be about just filling someone with facts or skills. That never works. The quest for leadership is a journey to discover who we are—to find the leader within us. Leadership is not a destination, but rather a long and satisfying journey. This journey is the Leadership Continuum: a continuous cycle of experience, reflection, intervention, and self-development that builds within us the confidence needed to lead.

Leadership is not a destination, but rather a long and satisfying journey.

Figure 1. *The In Pursuit of Leadership Model*

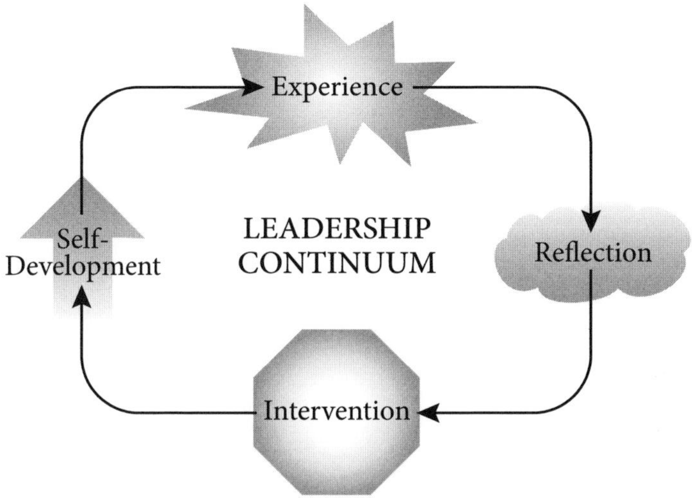

The *In Pursuit of Leadership Model* helps us visualize the Leadership Continuum, where leaders build in experiences, reflect on their actions, and develop strategies for intervention that lead to the self-development that strengthens their Character Equation and Leadership Formula.

Chapter 1

CHARACTER MATTERS!

Start with yourself first! And then go out from there.
Don't try to teach mathematics until
you've learned it yourself.
—John P. Kotter

IN 1980, I ENTERED the United States Military Academy at West Point as an 18-year-old new cadet, known as a "plebe." On our first day, all new cadets were issued *Bugle Notes*. This small 3" x 5" hardcover book has been given to plebes since 1907.

Bugle Notes serve as a basic training manual and contains essential knowledge for the new cadets. On page 68 of *Bugle Notes*, the Office of the Commandant defines the first mission of the academy this way:

> "To develop the qualities and attributes of leadership with emphasis on character as exemplified by integrity, morality, discipline, and a strong sense of duty and responsibility."

In short, the academy's mission is to develop leaders of character. I remember pondering the statement, "Not just leaders, but leaders of character." Of course, I'd heard about character long before I read my *Bugle Notes*, but I realized that I didn't truly understand what it meant.

What is Character?

As a leader, why do I need character? And if character is important, how do I improve it? The reason these questions are important is because in order to lead others, we must first lead ourselves. Leadership is first who we are, and then what we must be. The leadership process is leading out of the leader within. Therefore, leadership starts with the values and attributes or character traits that shape us as leaders.

Character is trait-neutral. We all have good and bad character traits. It's the net effect of our good and bad traits that defines our character. This is what I call the Character Equation.

Character = Good Traits + Bad Traits

If good traits outweigh bad traits, the result is a strong Character Equation. On the other hand, if bad traits outweigh good traits, the result is a weak Character Equation. It goes without saying that effective leaders have a strong Character Equation.

I believe it's our character that drives our behavior. With thoughtful reflection on our behavior, the outcome of our character, we can begin to understand our Character Equation. When we understand it, we can intervene to improve it. In this way, character building is viewed as a deliberate and progressive process that requires a continual cycle of reflection and intervention.

When we focus day in and day out on this important process of reflection and intervention, we can build and strengthen good character traits and also work to weaken or defeat our bad character traits. This is important because our true character often shows in the heat of the moment, before we have time to think. That is what makes your Character Equation so crucial.

Reflection and Intervention

In order to stack our Character Equation in our favor, we need to first consciously identify our character traits. We must understand ourselves. This is where personal reflection becomes very important.

Reflection, for many of us, is not natural. With the press of today's fast pace lifestyle, who has time to stop and look back? But this is exactly what is required in character building. If we believe our character is a dynamic force rather than a static force, we can begin to look honestly at our behavior and assess gaps between the current state and the ideal state. These gaps are our opportunities to improve. Effective leaders continually look for opportunities to "close the gaps." In other words, if we believe we lack or want to strengthen certain good character traits, we will incorporate daily opportunities to exercise the desired behavior or trait. In the same way, if we think our behavior is the result of bad character traits, we can intervene to weaken or defeat them. This all seems so incredibly simple, but the reality is that most people are not willing to make an honest assessment of their character and take the steps necessary to improve it.

Intervention requires discipline. It may be easy to identify a bad character trait, but it's difficult to defeat it. I think the natural tendency is to neglect our bad character traits, saying, "Oh, that's just part of my personality." Or, "I am so much better than that other person." This is really where character building starts. Leaders must continually analyze their behavior. If you can't be honest with yourself, you will never be able to accurately assess your strengths and weaknesses and, consequently, be unable to determine which areas need improvement. Without honest and continual assessment, followed by action for improvement, you will stagnate and fall behind.

Leaders must continually analyze their behavior.

For example, being responsible is a good character trait. Responsibility is realizing that you have control over your thoughts, feelings, and actions, and that you are accountable for your actions. If, upon reflection, you realize that you are often making excuses for your mistakes, you need to make a conscious effort to intervene—to close the gap. In the future, you can make a conscious effort to own up to your mistakes.

You cannot get to where you want to be by staying where you are. Character is not built into us. Character is built from within us. Character development is the process of closing the gap between our current character and our ideal character. I like the analogy of an archer shooting an arrow at a target. An effective archer doesn't just look up at the target and let the arrow fly. They take aim, shoot an arrow, assess the shot, and make adjustments until they hit the mark consistently. Our beliefs shape our character. If we believe we need to change, and accept the work it will require to do so, we are likely to practice that change until it becomes a reality. This reflection on our behavior gives us the opportunity to build the character within that was once thought to be ambiguous and unreachable. In the end, building character is a choice.

Character is not built into us. Character is built from within us.

Building Character

I played high school hockey in White Bear Lake, Minnesota. After 45 minutes of grueling wind sprints on an outdoor ice rink next to the school, I remember my hockey coach telling our team: "There you go boys. That's character building. How did you do?" At that time, I didn't find the connection between challenging physical training in practice and character building. This is where coaches and leaders make the most impact: They educate us about the *process* of building character. It is the leader's responsibility to provide the team with character-building opportunities.

By making the team skate wind sprints long after our legs were dead tired, my high school hockey coach gave us the opportunity to learn about the character of our team and, more importantly, our own character. He was trying to instill in us good team and personal character traits like: commitment, perseverance, and esprit de corps. For example, he taught us commitment by making us do them together as a team. He taught us perseverance by challenging us to keep going even when we were beyond tired and wanted to quit. He taught us esprit de corps by bonding together in the warming house after it was over, feeling both exhausted and content. Coach allowed us to recognize in ourselves and in our teammates, areas for improvement and used these examples as teaching points. For example, in order to gain unfair advantage, skaters did not stop on the lines. Our coach called them out by saying, "Don't cheat your teammates. Stop on the lines." In the end, he never used wind sprints as punishment. Coach used wind sprints in a positive way as conditioning and, more importantly, as a tool to reveal our character and the need to make choices to improve it.

Coaches are first and foremost teachers. They can be very influential people in the lives of their players. Because they are such powerful role models, players often learn more from them about character than about athletic performance.

For me, it wasn't until my later years at West Point and as an officer in the U. S. Army that I began to realize how much character mattered. It was also during this time that I discovered that character drives our actions and behaviors. More importantly, I learned that character building is a process that can be improved through reflection and intervention. Now that you have a better understanding of why character matters, begin an honest assessment of your Character Equation. Look for other people demonstrating the positive character traits you desire and work to build them into your life.

Sports do not build character, they reveal it.
—John Wooden, legendary basketball coach

Character Trumps Talent

The reason character matters is because I believe it plays a big role in success. I define success or the ability to win in one simple equation:

Ability to Win = Character x Talent

Character and talent are the two key variables that determine the ability to win. One without the other brings only half success. It isn't enough to just be talented. You must have the right character. There is no doubt that talent is important, of course, but in many cases it is God-given talent. When analyzing players with equal talent level, the ones who stand out as top performers have the most character—the most will to win. When they face adversity, these top performers work harder and demonstrate a greater ability to concentrate.

> *Someone with greater heart can outperform someone with greater talent.*

The good news is that it doesn't take great skills to have great heart. Like a diamond, character is formed through time and pressure. Over the years, I have found that character and heart are perhaps the most important measures for success. Someone with greater heart could outperform someone with greater talent. Winning is more than an equation—it is a process. And like most processes, it can be improved through hard work and intentionality.

You Gotta Have Heart

I coached youth hockey for many years in both the Chicago and Minneapolis areas. Before the season, I asked my players one by one, "Do you want to win?" Invariably, they all said yes. Then I told them, "Wanting to win means nothing. Everyone wants to win. The other team wants to win too. You have to have the will to win." Then I told them how Wayne Gretzky learned this lesson after the final game of his 1983 season.

In 1983, with high hopes after a great regular season, the Edmonton Oilers entered their first Stanley Cup playoffs. They breezed to the finals by defeating the Winnipeg Jets 3 games to 0 (In 1983, the Division semi-finals were a 5-game series), the Calgary Flames 4 games to 1, and the Chicago Blackhawks 4 games to 0. In eliminating these teams, the Oilers had won 11 of 12 games and outscored their opponents 74 to 33, averaging over 6 goals a game. In the finals, they faced off against the three-time defending champion, the New York

Islanders. This was the Oilers' big chance to win their first Stanley Cup. This was Gretzky's chance to become the "Great One," something people were already starting to call him.

The Oilers got swept 4 games to 0 with Gretzky getting a total of 0 goals! In Gretzky's own words, "Their big four—Bossy, Trottier, Potvin, and Smith—danced all over us, Smith (the goalie) especially. He slashed, dove, screamed, whatever it took. He was so fantastic they gave him the Conn Smyth trophy as MVP."

After the final game, Gretzky and his teammate, Kevin Lowe, knew they had to walk past the Islanders' locker room on the way to their bus. They were bracing for the happy faces, champagne, and celebrating that go with winning the Stanley Cup. What they saw on their walk to the bus had an amazing impact on them. Wives, girlfriends, coaches, and staff were celebrating, but the players were not. The Islanders were completely exhausted. Trottier was icing a swollen knee, Potvin was getting a shoulder rub down, and numerous other players were limping around with black eyes and bleeding mouths. In Gretzky's words:

> "It looked more like a morgue in there than a champion's locker room. And here we were, perfectly healthy. That's why they won and we lost. They took more punishment than we did. They dove into more

> boards, stuck their faces in front of more pucks, threw their bodies into more pile ups. They sacrificed everything they had. And that's when Kevin said something to me I'll never forget. He said, *That's how you win championships.*"

Gretzky and the Oilers wanted to win, but the Islanders had the greater will to win. Both teams had great talent, but the 1983 Islanders had more character. In the end, their character made the difference.

The Harder Right

It was the end of my junior year. Classes were over and we were waiting for our summer duty assignments to start. It was always my favorite time of year at West Point. With no more school, there was plenty of time to explore the academy grounds with a clear mind. One of my favorite places to go was the Cadet Chapel.

The Cadet Chapel is on the hill up from the main campus and dominates the skyline. It was completed in 1910 and serves as a bastion for many cadets seeking some solace from their often chaotic, fast-paced lives. It was during the spring of my junior year in the Cadet Chapel that I started to understand the meaning of character.

During my first three years at the Academy, with chapel services filled with worshippers, I had recited the Cadet Prayer many times—so many times that I had it memorized. However, that spring, while sitting alone in the empty chapel, a three-sentence section in the middle of the prayer caught my attention in a fresh, new way:

> "Encourage us in our endeavor to live above the common level of life. Make us to choose the harder right instead of the easier wrong, and never be content with a half truth when the whole can be won. Endow us with courage that is born of loyalty to all that is noble and worthy, that scorns to compromise with vice and injustice and knows no fear when truth and right are in jeopardy."

I thought, *This must be how leaders of character aspire to act.* It finally started to make sense to me—actions define character. It helped me realize that character is ultimately a choice.

Actions Define Character

An individual's character often shows through in the spur of the moment, when quick thinking is required. Recently, a pastor told a story about a confirmation service that demonstrates how actions are a direct result of our character.

In the Lutheran faith, confirmation is very important. It is a public profession of faith by teenage girls and boys who have gone through long and careful instruction. This process culminates with a customary confirmation service attended by family and friends. On the occasion of this particular confirmation service at a large suburban Lutheran church, the entire class of confirmation students knelt before the alter. The pastor invited the parents, grandparents, godparents, and friends to come down to the alter and place their hands of prayerful support on their confirmee's shoulder. A few moments later, all the students had large support groups behind them—all but one.

One young boy knelt down, all alone. No parents, grandparents, godparents, nor friends stood behind him. An usher at the back of the church quietly rushed down the main aisle to the alter, stood behind the boy, and placed his hand on the boy's shoulder.

Many years later, the boy, now a grown man with a family, recognized the pastor at a local shopping mall. He introduced himself and asked if the man was indeed the pastor at the confirmation service so many years ago. The pastor answered, "Yes I am."

The man replied, "On that confirmation day, the usher's gesture of support changed my life."

In the spur of the moment, the usher's actions revealed his true character. Both leadership and the winning equation start with character. However, defining character can be difficult because without a certain amount of introspection, it is an impossible task. Character can be developed. The first step is to look inside to identify your Character Equation. Then look outside for opportunities to improve it. The character development process is both deliberate and progressive. This continuous cycle of personal reflection and intervention is critical.

An individual's character often shows through in the spur of the moment.

A Final Note on Character

In May 1991, a few months before his retirement, General Norman Schwarzkopf returned to West Point, his Alma mater, to address the Corps of Cadets. In this address, he spoke about the requirements to be leaders in the 21st century:

> "To be a 21st-century leader, you must have two things: competence and character. I've met a lot of leaders that were very, very, very competent. But they didn't have character. For every job they did well in the Army, they sought rewards in the form of promotions, in the form of awards and decorations, in the form of getting ahead at the expense of somebody else, in the form of another piece of paper that awarded them some degree. The only reasons why they wanted that was because it was a sure road to faster promotion, to somehow get to the top. You see, these were very competent people, but they lacked character.
>
> Now, on the other hand, I've met a lot of leaders who had superb character, but they weren't willing to hold their own feet to the fire. They weren't willing to pay the price of leadership. They were not willing to go the extra mile, to do that extra little bit because that's what it took to be a great leader.

> I've seen competent leaders who stood in front of a platoon and saw it as a platoon. But I've seen great leaders who stood in front of a platoon and saw it as 44 individuals, each of whom had his hopes, each of whom had his aspirations, each of whom wanted to live. Each of whom wanted to do good. So you must have competence and you must have character. Some great man once said character is seen only when nobody is watching. It's not what people do when they are being watched that demonstrates character; it's what they do when they are not being watched that demonstrated true character."

The most poignant part of General Schwarzkopf's quote is his emphasis on competent leaders who were not willing to pay the price for leadership. Improving your Character Equation doesn't just happen because you want it to. It happens because you are willing to go the extra mile to find opportunities to improve it. In the end, character development is a choice.

As the likes of Wayne Gretzky, General Norman Schwarzkopf, and UCLA Coach John Wooden learned through experience, it takes a strong will to find success in life. That will to win gets at the heart of character. It defines the work ethic, perseverance, courage, commitment, and esprit de corps that, along with God-given talent, make up the winning equation. Effective leadership requires a strong Character Equation!

Chapter One Summary
Character Matters!

Character Equation:

Character = (Good Traits + Bad Traits)

- Character is not built into us, character is built from within us.
- First look inside to find your Character Equation, then look outside for opportunities to strengthen it.
- Close the gap between current character and ideal character.

The Winning Equation:

Ability to Win = Character x Talent

- Character trumps talent.
- It doesn't take great skills to have great heart.
- Character drives behavior.

Exercise One

Character Equation Worksheet

OBJECTIVE: Apply the *In Pursuit of Leadership Model* to selected character traits to improve your Character Equation.

Figure 1. **In Pursuit of Leadership Model**

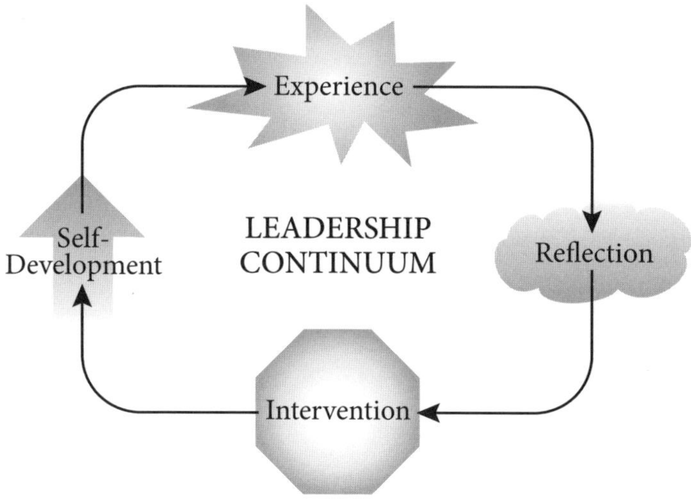

EXAMPLE: Mahatma Gandhi is often described as a man of character. This story from his youth displays strength of character and is useful for identifying character traits: At the age of fifteen, Gandhi stole a piece of gold from his brother.

As time went on, the burden of this sin was too high for him to bear and he decided to admit it. He wrote down what happened on a sheet of paper and gave it to his father. In the note, he confessed his guilt and asked for punishment. In his autobiography, Gandhi wrote, "I had thought that he would be angry, say harsh words and strike his forehead. But he was so wonderfully peaceful, and this was due to my confession."

This story presents a number of character traits: honesty, courage, and forgiveness, for example. Think of your own journey and find experiences that define *your* character traits.

TASK: Take some time to reflect on your most recent behaviors to help determine where to rank yourself on each attribute. Look at each character trait on the following page and circle the number you think most closely matches your current level. Be completely honest with this self-assessment.

Our actions reveal to us our character. By reflecting on our actions, we can develop conscious strategies for intervention. This intervention leads to the self-development that strengthens our character. New experiences lead to new actions and the cycle continues.

Character Traits Worksheet

Circle the number you think most closely matches your current level.

Courage

1 (low) 2 3 4 5 6 7 8 9 10 (high)

Honesty

1 (low) 2 3 4 5 6 7 8 9 10 (high)

Tolerance

1 (low) 2 3 4 5 6 7 8 9 10 (high)

Self-discipline

1 (low) 2 3 4 5 6 7 8 9 10 (high)

Humility

1 (low) 2 3 4 5 6 7 8 9 10 (high)

Forgiveness

1 (low) 2 3 4 5 6 7 8 9 10 (high)

Compassion

1 (low) 2 3 4 5 6 7 8 9 10 (high)

Competence

1 (low) 2 3 4 5 6 7 8 9 10 (high)

Will

1 (low) 2 3 4 5 6 7 8 9 10 (high)

Flexibility

1 (low) 2 3 4 5 6 7 8 9 10 (high)

Confidence

1 (low) 2 3 4 5 6 7 8 9 10 (high)

Loyalty

1 (low) 2 3 4 5 6 7 8 9 10 (high)

Teamwork

1 (low) 2 3 4 5 6 7 8 9 10 (high)

Commitment

1 (low) 2 3 4 5 6 7 8 9 10 (high)

Sincerity

1 (low) 2 3 4 5 6 7 8 9 10 (high)

From the Character Traits Worksheet on the previous pages, fill in the following:

Weaknesses (the two traits with the lowest numbers):

1. ____

2. ____

Strengths (the two traits with the highest numbers):

1. ____

2. ____

Strategies for Moving Forward

Apply the *In Pursuit of Leadership Model* to the list above to improve your Character Equation. Remember, self-development begins with reflection.

- Work on your positive traits first. Strengthen them.
- Turn weaknesses into strengths. This works both sides of the Character Equation at the same time.
- Write down two traits that you want to strengthen. Keep them handy. At the end of each day for one month, reflect on them and ask yourself: Did I strengthen them today?

- Continually look for opportunities to strengthen your Character Equation and take action! Remember, you can't get to where you want to be by staying where you are.

Future Exercises

- Mark your calendar for six months. Go to www.InPursuitofLeadership.com to download the Character Traits Worksheet and complete it. Notice any differences and use the *In Pursuit of Leadership Model* to repeat the self-development exercise.
- Mark your calendar for one year. Download and complete the Character Traits Worksheet once again. Notice any differences from your original worksheet and the one you took six months later. Use the *In Pursuit of Leadership Model* to repeat the self-development exercise.

Character cannot be developed in ease and quiet. Only through the experience of trial and suffering can the soul be strengthened, vision cleared, ambition inspired, and success achieved.

—Helen Keller

Chapter 2

LEADERSHIP TAKES TIME

Leadership is an art,
something to be learned over time,
not simply from reading books.
—Max De Pree

WHEN I LOOK BACK NOW at my experience at West Point, the idea of learning to follow and obey before leading and commanding makes sense to me. However, during my first year there, at the bottom of the pyramid and away from the security of high school and home, I had many occasions to wonder, *Who am I?* This struck me after getting my first plebe haircut, looking in the mirror and seeing a totally foreign, hairless person looking back at me. Understanding and accepting my role as a follower took time.

Mary Louise Menikheim from the Centre for Applied Leadership, makes the point, "To become a leader, one must first serve an apprenticeship as a courageous follower." It only makes sense that leaders appointed without sufficient experience in positions of followership have a difficult road ahead of them. In fact, their appointers have done them no favors.

Leaders without sufficient experience as followers have a difficult road.

Learning to be an effective follower in order to be an effective leader is not a new concept. For over 100 years, the United State Military Academy at West Point has been using a model to establish followership that helps cadets move through this important leadership development process.

In his book, *The West Point Way of Leadership*, Larry R. Donnithorne explains how cadets embark on four phases of leadership training:

The First Pass:

- Forging bonds that hold the organization together
- Emphasizing teamwork and absorbing an institution's value system

The Second Pass:

- Positioning the individual inside the group
- Helping individuals begin to find their voice in the organization by emphasizing direct or face-to-face leadership

The Third Pass:

- Acquiring the self-reliance to lead leaders
- Teaching the skills necessary for indirect leadership or leading people who lead people

The Fourth Pass:

- Serving as the organization's eyes and ears
- Developing skills necessary for executive leadership or how to act in their organization's long-term interest

Before allowing new cadets the chance to find their own voice through direct or face-to-face leadership in the second phase, they must work their way through the first phase, which emphasizes teamwork and allows time for absorbing and appreciating an institution's value system. This is a very important rite of passage. Cadets pass through an entire year observing leaders. By following, they learn from their leader's successes and failures. Before they are even allowed to express their own voices, they listen to the voices of the leaders around them.

What makes the cadet's experience as a follower so valuable is that his or her leaders are with them from the time they get up in the morning until the time they retire to their rooms at night. This is why direct leadership is so important to the follower. Direct leaders are close enough for followers to see first-hand how leadership techniques succeed and fail. This idea of learning through phases places more emphasis on the learning process, building on a body of knowledge over time. The entire concept of time-phased leadership development takes into consideration the tremendous value of followership. It also supports that leadership, like any skill, can be developed with practice and hard work.

The Leadership Formula: Art and Science

You attend a conference and the keynote speaker is introduced. Their credentials are impressive and accomplishments awesome. You take note as the speaker steps forward. The presentation is strong. You are inspired. As you leave the conference, you think to yourself, *Wow. There it is. That's leadership.* But as you sit down at your desk the next day, you notice an uneasy feeling deep down inside and realize, *This is not that simple.* Suddenly, it becomes clear to you that leadership doesn't come with the birth certificate, nor does it come with the job. You begin to appreciate the complexity of the leadership process and, more importantly, the limitations of your own leadership experience. At this point, you realize that there's much more to leadership than meets the eye.

In Minnesota, to become a millwright, you must first complete 8,000 hours of work with a qualified journeyperson and attend trade school. This apprenticeship program is 90% on-the-job and 10% classroom training. Clearly, the transition from apprentice to journeyperson tells us a couple key points: 1) you must be a follower first, and 2) the process takes time to complete. This dedication to both art and science is true with most artisan trades whose origins predate the Industrial Revolution. However, this commitment to on-the-job training and devotion for the science of the trade does not reflect the common approach to leadership. On the contrary, there seems to be a common belief that leadership comes with the position. Unfortunately, the only thing that comes with the position is the title. Everything else is earned.

The experiences and knowledge acquired on our leadership journey translate into a unique set of skills.

Art is an expression of what is beautiful or appealing. It is also described as skilled workmanship or a craft, as in arts and crafts. More specifically, when we view leadership as art, we see it as inherent skills derived from our personal attributes, values, beliefs, and experiences. As we travel on our leadership journey, our experiences and acquired knowledge translate into a unique set of skills. It is also important to recognize that what we learn from our past experiences is limited because our experiences are limited.

Science is knowledge gained by systematic study. When we view leadership as science, it represents a set of conceptual frameworks derived from systematic study. Emerging leaders tend to be drawn to the science of leadership because it is something concrete that they can study, describe, learn, try, and measure. Some never delve into the artistic side of leadership because it is less tangible and less emphasized by professors and mentors.

These two sides of leadership (art and science) should not be viewed in conflict.

These two sides of leadership (art and science) should not be viewed in conflict. Studying the science of leadership gives us the capability to understand the individual components that comprise good leadership. Studying the art of leadership helps us understand and value the personal contribution our strengths and attributes can make to our leadership journey.

We all start at different points on the leadership curve. In other words, we all start our leadership journeys at individual skill levels that are not equally handed out at birth. Each leader's formula is different. Levels of practical experiences and theoretical study are unique to the individual. The sum of these two factors equals their Leadership Formula:

Practical Experience
x Theoretical Experience
= Leadership

Both factors can be improved over time by more leadership experience and more study. The more experiences we engage in, the more opportunities we have to improve our Leadership Formula. Dwight Eisenhower wrote, "I realize that leadership is to some extent a gift, but no one can tell me that the gifts a person has—whatever they may be—cannot be *improved by study of historical examples and effective leadership methods.*" Ultimately, these experiences allow us to grow the leader within us.

Be A Follower First

A good leader is first a good subordinate. To support this important leadership principle, we only need to study the careers of two famous American leaders: Robert E. Lee and Dwight D. Eisenhower. Both men served long military careers in supporting staff positions before having the opportunity to lead troops in battle. In addition, both men served apprenticeships as staff officers under accomplished generals, who served as their leadership mentors and provided profound leadership educational experiences.

A good leader is first a good subordinate.

During their leadership journeys, Lee and Eisenhower both experienced difficult apprenticeships that strengthened their character, culminating in a rite of passage that challenged their leadership skills. Whether you have a natural bent toward studying history or not, I guarantee you will benefit from reading about the leadership journeys of these two men in our great American history. All leaders must endure a rite of passage—a trial by fire. Like character, leadership is best challenged and, therefore, defined under fire. These challenges transform a potential leader into an active leader, justify a leader to those they lead and, most importantly, give credibility and confidence to the leader. For Lee and Eisenhower, this rite of passage confirmed their transition from follower to leader and prepared them to meet future leadership challenges.

The Leadership of Robert E. Lee

Robert E. Lee graduated from West Point in 1829. Until the start of the Mexican-American War in 1846, Lee worked as an engineer. After the war, excluding his time as the Superintendent at West Point, he served in staff positions. Lee's first direct leadership role came in 1856, as second in command of a cavalry regiment. He was 56 years old. Five years later at the Civil War Battle of Cheat Mountain, at the age of 61, Lee finally led troops into battle for the first time.

Lee's Years of Apprenticeship: 1834–1861

Robert E. Lee served a particularly long apprenticeship in the army that began in the fall of 1834 when he was assigned to the Corps of Engineers headquarters in Washington D.C. As a lieutenant, in the summer of 1835, he worked on mapping the state line between Ohio and Michigan and in 1837, supervised engineering work for St. Louis harbor and other projects on the upper Mississippi and Missouri rivers. In July

1838, Lee was promoted Captain and continued his work primarily on inspection tours to corps sites and civil engineering projects. In the spring of 1841, Lee was assigned as Post Engineer at Fort Hamilton in Brooklyn, New York. He remained there until 1846.

Over the years, Lee won recognition for excellence among the army's engineers and in July 1844 was appointed to a board of officers to attend the West Point final examinations. It was on this distinguished board that Lee met Winfield Scott who would become his leadership mentor.

With the outbreak of war with Mexico in 1846, Lee was assigned as a staff engineer under Brigadier General John E. Wool. In this position, he directed the building and repair of roads and bridges from San Antonio, Texas to Saltillo, Mexico. In January 1847, Lee received orders to report to Major General Winfield Scott, commanding general of the U.S. Army, as chief engineer of the main army of invasion. Lee joined Scott in Brazos, Texas and from there they prepared an amphibious assault of Mexico at Veracruz, the first large scale amphibious landing by U.S. military forces. This landing ended with the surrender of the city and paved the way for their victorious assault on Mexico City. General Scott was made a national hero for his victorious campaign and under his watchful eye, Lee had performed exceptionally.

After the war, in 1848, Lee returned to Washington and resumed duties in the corps headquarters until he was named the Superintendent at West Point in May 1852. He held that post until September 1855. With vast quantities of land acquired from Mexico after the war, Congress authorized the establishment of new cavalry regiments. In the spring of 1856, at 49 years old, Lieutenant Colonel Robert E. Lee arrived at Camp Cooper to command two Squadrons of the newly formed 2nd U.S. Cavalry Regiment. This regiment was known as "Jeff Davis's Own," after Jefferson Davis, the secretary of war for President Franklin Pierce. They were an elite organization commanded by Colonel Albert S. Johnston, who went on to become the highest ranking Confederate general until he was killed at the Civil War Battle of Shiloh.

Camp Cooper was located on the Comanche reservation 25 miles north of Albany, Texas. It was a lonely station and Lee adapted himself to supervising routine post life. During this time he had the chance to develop his leadership craft and lead troops in a relatively safe environment. Besides a short time in 1859, while on leave of absence in Virginia leading a detachment of U. S. Marines to suppress John Brown and his abolitionist raiders at Harpers Ferry, Lee would not lead men in battle until early in the Civil War.

In 1861, his mentor General Winfield Scott ordered Lee back to Washington to take on greater responsibility in the expanding Union Army in preparation to fight the Southern states that had left the Union. To Scott's surprise, Lee resigned. Instead Lee took up command of the Virginia state forces. It is ironic that Lee turned down the command offered to him by his mentor General Scott, who he had so loyally served as a scout and staff officer during the Mexican–American War. Now, as a Confederate General, Lee would potentially fight against his mentor. It was during the early stages of the Civil War that Lee experienced the rite of passage that all emerging leaders face.

Lee's Rite of Passage

In September of 1861, during the early stages of Civil War, Lee was appointed by Confederate President, Jefferson Davis, to command all of Virginia's forces. In his first time leading troops in battle, Lee struggled and suffered a defeat at the Battle of Cheat Mountain in western Virginia. The following month, he was sent to organize defenses along the South Carolina, Georgia, and the eastern Florida coastlines.

In the Deep South, Lee was unable to endear himself to local leaders, who were not impressed with his battle record in western Virginia. Lee was forced to make difficult decisions and without the support of local leaders and plantation owners, was unable to accomplish the defensive measures as quickly as he hoped. Lee's critics viewed him as too cautious and gave him the nickname, "Granny Lee." They argued that he may be a great military theorist, staff officer, and engineer, but he was unsuited to lead troops in combat. Luckily for Lee, Jefferson Davis did not agree with Lee's critics and recalled him back to Richmond to be his military advisor.

While in Richmond, Lee was ridiculed for ordering excessive trench digging around the Confederate capitol and earned the nickname, "King of Spades." However, in the face of this adversity and self-doubt, not unlike most new leaders feel, Lee remained loyal to President Jefferson. Lee waited for his next opportunity to show leadership. He would not have to wait long. In June 1862, at the Battle of Seven Pines, Confederate General Joseph E. Johnston was wounded, and Lee assumed command of the Army of Northern Virginia. This was Lee's first opportunity to lead an army in the field.

The Confederate press objected to Lee's appointment, echoing the lack of support Lee found months earlier while in the Deep South. They feared Lee would not be aggressive enough to stop the advance of General George B. McClellan's Union Army of the Potomac, who during the Peninsula Campaign had moved from Fort Monroe up the Virginia Peninsula to the eastern edges of Richmond. As McClellan planned for a siege and capture of Richmond, Lee launched an aggressive offensive and seized the strategic initiative.

In what became known as the Seven Days Battles, Lee drove the Union Army back to the James River and saved the Confederate capitol. These successful battles quickly changed public opinion and now newspapers lauded Lee's aggressiveness. These battles marked the turning point in Lee's leadership journey. This was the beginning of Lee's legend. From now until the end of the war, his troops would affectionately refer to him as "The Old Man" or "Marse Lee" (Marse slang for "Master")

After McClellan's retreat, Lee led his army north against Union General John Pope's Army of Virginia at the Second Battle of Bull Run. Lee's army defeated the Union forces and pushed them out of Virginia. This was a huge moral victory for the Confederacy. In just 90 days of taking command of the Confederate Army, Lee had saved Richmond, ended the Confederate retreat, and driven the Union Army back to within 20 miles of their own capitol, Washington. Instead of the quick end to the war that McClellan's Peninsula Campaign promised, the war went on for almost another three years.

Robert E. Lee went into the Mexican War as an apprentice and left it as a professional officer; however, it would be another 14 years before he would lead troops in battle. These were difficult times for Lee. He even contemplated leaving the Army and returning to his home in Virginia. When the Civil War finally did start, all the years of leadership development served him well. Lee was prepared. He successfully met the challenge of his leadership rite of passage and went on to become one of the great leaders in American history.

The Leadership of Dwight D. Eisenhower

Like Robert E. Lee, Dwight D. Eisenhower, or "Ike," as he is commonly referred to, served in the army many years before he assumed his first direct leadership position. Also like Lee, Ike served a lengthy leadership apprenticeship on the staff of some of the Army's greatest generals, where he observed and learned first-hand the art of leadership.

In April 1917, when the United States entered World War I, Ike was at Fort Sam Houston in San Antonio, Texas, training the newly-formed 57th Infantry Regiment. By February 1918,

Ike was assigned to Camp Meade, Maryland, to organize and train the new 301st Tank Battalion, which was planning to go to the battlefields of France in the spring. However, much to his chagrin, Ike was reassigned to the newly created tank training center at Camp Colt, which was established to conduct preliminary training for tank soldiers before going overseas for combat. Ike assumed command in March of 1918. By November, the Germans had signed the Armistice to end the war, which also ended Ike's brief command. He was 28 years old when World War I ended. After the war, he was deflated and disappointed. By no fault of his own, he had missed being a part of the action in the greatest war in history.

Ike's Years of Apprenticeship: 1919–1941

In 1922, in the Panama Canal Zone as the 25th Infantry Brigade Executive Officer under General Fox Connor, Ike began his leadership apprenticeship. In fact, it was from Connor that Ike first heard about Major George C. Marshall, who later became the first American general to be promoted to the five-star rank. Marshall served under Connor on General John J. Pershing's staff during the successful Argonne-Meuse Offensive, the final Allied offensive of World War I. Many years later, in a bold and somewhat controversial decision, Marshall selected Ike to lead the allied invasion of Europe.

While in Panama, General Connor inspired a new dedication in Ike and tutored him on military history. Ike turned the second-story porch of their home into a military history workroom, where he studied the French military strategy masters. Under Connor's tutelage, Ike read Napoleon's memoirs, Jomini's commentaries on Napoleonic strategy, Ardant du Picq's *Battle Studies*, Foch's *The Principles of War*, and the great German military theorist Clausewitz's *On War*. American, Denis Hart Mahan, also had a lasting impact on Ike.

Mahan was a West Point graduate who taught at the Academy from 1832 to 1871. Mahan's book, *Elementary Treatise of Advanced-Guard, Out-post, and Detachment Service of Troops* was America's first comprehensive study of tactics and strategy. In this book, Mahan wrote: "How different is almost every military problem, except in the bare mechanism of tactics…Too often the general has only conjectures to go on, and these based upon false premises…(For) what is true now, at the next moment may have no existence, or exist in the contrary sense." Although greatly influenced by classic military theory, it is clear that Mahan favored flexible pragmatism over the heavy reliance on systems and laws as applied by the Europeans, in particular the Germans like Clausewitz. Mahan believed that war was more a matter of art than science. This concept made a lasting impact on Ike and helped shape the path of his military career. It was Connor who took Eisenhower under his wing and helped him attend the Command and General Staff College at Fort Leavenworth, Kansas.

In August 1925, Ike reported for duty at the Command and General Staff College. The origins of the college date back to 1881 when Commanding General of the United Sates Army, William Tecumseh Sherman, ordered the establishment of the School of Application for Infantry and Cavalry. As the name indicates, it was a school to train officers in the fundamentals of military operations, tactics, and logistics of large army units. The Command and General Staff College was a very competitive and stressful experience. Ike was in direct competition with 275 of the best officers in the Army, who had all been handpicked by their superiors. The school was designed to discover not only who had the brains, but also who could take the strain. Ike did well in this environment and graduated first in his class. His apprenticeship under Connor had paid off. It would be Fox Connor again who would have a hand in Ike's next assignment to the American Battle Monuments Commission, in Washington, D.C.

In January 1927, Ike reported to the commission. His challenge, during this short assignment, was to prepare for General Pershing a guidebook on the battlefields of World War I.

The commission wanted a book of convenient size, which the Government Printing Office could sell for seventy-five cents. However, they wanted it completed in just six months. Ike rose to the challenge and produced *A Guide to the American Battle Fields of Europe*. Ike had met his timeline and the book was printed that fall. It was well received by General Pershing. This fateful assignment was excellent preparation for Ike's eventual duties in World War II. As a reward, Pershing and Connor helped Ike with his next assignment, admission to the Army War College.

Located in the 1920's along the Potomac River in downtown Washington, the Army War College was a pleasant, contemplative assignment for senior professionals of that generation. It was in this atmosphere that Major Eisenhower entered with the academic class of 1927–1928. The War College provided a much more academic and leisurely respite setting---a different setting from the pressures of the Command and General Staff College. Ike graduated in 1928. After the War College, General Pershing wanted to revise the popular guidebook Ike had completed earlier. Ike accepted the assignment with the American Battle Monuments Commission, but this time travelled to France. This gave him the opportunity for first-hand visits to the battlefields in Europe that he initially wrote about using only maps.

After his assignment with the commission, Eisenhower returned to the United States and began a series of staff positions in Washington D.C., California, and Texas. The most important of these assignments was working as chief military aide to General MacArthur. In 1935, he accompanied MacArthur to the Philippines, where he served as Assistant Military Advisor. In 1936, after an incredible 16 years as a major, he was promoted to Lieutenant Colonel. He was 46 years old and had no combat experience and only very brief command experience many years earlier at Camp Colt in Gettysburg, Pennsylvania. From here on out, things would move quickly for Ike.

Eisenhower returned to the United States in 1939 and in March 1941, he became a full colonel. In June 1941, he was appointed Chief of Staff to General Krueger, Commander of the 3rd Army located at Fort Sam Houston, Texas. In September 1941, on the eve of the bombing of Pearl Harbor, he was promoted to Brigadier General. In December 1941, when war on Japan and Germany was declared, Ike was on his way to Washington D.C to become the Assistant Chief of War Plans under General Marshall, who had just implemented a major restructuring of the War Department. During this period, although Ike didn't know it, Marshall was closely measuring his performance. In April 1942, Marshall appointed him to

Assistant Chief of Staff Operations Division. In just two more months, Ike would be on his way to England to assume command of the European Theater of Operations. Although he had demonstrated excellent administrative and staff duties, he had virtually no command experience, and no combat experience. On June 24, 1942, when Ike stepped off the plane in England, he stepped into his leadership rite to passage. He was 51 years old.

Ike's Rite of Passage

As the European Theater Commander, Eisenhower's main duty was to prepare for the first joint British-American offensive since the French and Indian War. This offensive would eventually be the allied invasion of North Africa, code named Operation Torch. By November 1942, Ike had moved his headquarters to Gibraltar. It was his first time in a war zone. The first six months of 1942 would be the turning point of both the war and for the newly promoted General Eisenhower. The eyes of the allied command and now the whole world were watching.

1942 was a pivotal year during World War II. By August, Hitler's huge 6th Army reached Stalingrad. After a five-month siege, in an astonishing reversal, the Russians encircled and trapped their Nazi enemy. In October 1942, in North Africa, the British 8th Army, led by General Bernard Montgomery, delivered a crushing defeat of General Rommel's Afrika Korps at the battle of El Alamein. This battle, taken in conjunction with the German debacle at Stalingrad, proved strategically decisive and marked a clear turning of the tide against the German march of conquest.

In early November 1942, Eisenhower, just promoted to Supreme Commander Allied Expeditionary Force of the North Africa Theater of Operations, ordered the start of Operation Torch, an amphibious landing of North Africa. This huge operation would be a prelude to the cross-Channel attack at Normandy two years later. Operation Torch lasted six months, much longer than planned. Eisenhower's men fought hard and won. Perhaps Ike's biggest contribution was not leading the Anglo-American victory, but insisting that the allies had won it together. Thanks in large part to Eisenhower, the Alliance survived its first test and was stronger than ever.

In *Eisenhower 1890–1952*, author Stephen Ambrose writes, "In his first combat experience, Eisenhower was unsure of himself, hesitant, often depressed, irritable, liable to make snap judgments in insufficient information, defensive in both his mind and his tactics. Nineteen months later, he had improved dramatically and so had his superiors and subordinates. The team that invaded France in June 1944 was vastly superior to the team that invaded French North Africa in November 1942." Although a little rattled, Eisenhower successfully met the challenge of his leadership rite of passage and went on to be one of the great heroes of American history.

The leadership journeys of Lee and Ike serve as examples of leaders who distinguished themselves first as effective and courageous followers before they became effective leaders. Their long apprenticeships serving great leaders and learning the craft of leadership culminated in a rite of passage that confirmed their transition from follower to leader.

Leadership is a skill that can be developed with practice and hard work.

The transition from follower to leader is a difficult step. It always seems much easier to lead others…until you actually have to do it. But once you start this leadership journey, it is critical to know that leadership is the by-product of a process that combines both practical learning from our leadership experiences and the constant theoretical study of leadership principles. Ultimately, leadership is a skill that can be developed with practice and hard work. Acknowledge this challenge and commit yourself to this developmental process. This life-long process reminds us that leadership is a journey, not a destination.

Chapter Two Summary

Leadership Takes Time

Leadership Formula:

Practical Experience x Theoretical Experience = Leadership

- Leadership is both art and science.
- Learn the craft. Become a student of leadership.
- The more experiences we engage in, the more opportunities we have to improve our Leadership Formula.Leadership doesn't look for you; You need to look for it.

Followership is an Apprenticeship to Leadership

- A good leader is first a good follower.
- Leadership comes daily, not in a day.
- If you stop learning, you stop leading.

The *In Pursuit of Leadership Progression Model* depicts the leadership journey through followership, apprenticeship, and the challenging transition to direct leadership. This journey often includes leadership restarts, where a leader circles back to a follower role before moving back into a leadership role again.

Figure 2. **In Pursuit of Leadership Progression Model**

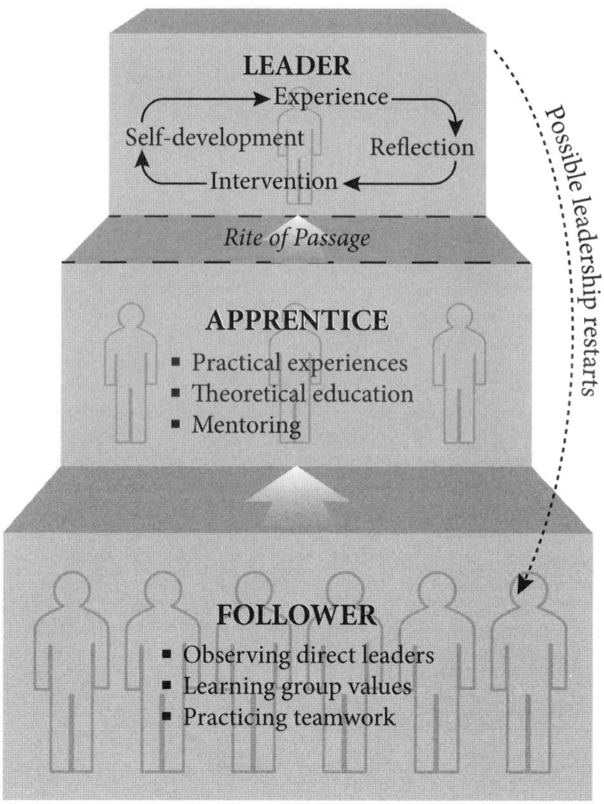

Exercise Two

Improve Your Leadership Formula

OBJECTIVE: Identify both practical and theoretical experiences and commit yourself to them. Become a student of leadership. Reflect on your experiences and reassess your Leadership Formula. Use the Leadership Formula to guide you and strengthen your leadership skills.

TASK: Take some time to identify actions that can provide for you both practical and theoretical experiences. Write them down in the spaces below.

Practical Experience	x	Theoretical Experience
____________________		____________________
____________________		____________________
____________________		____________________
____________________		____________________
____________________		____________________
____________________		____________________
____________________		____________________

Highlight an action from each side of the equation. Now go out and make it happen.

Strategies for Moving Forward

- Find a leadership mentor and make a connection.
- Expand your Practical Experiences by practicing the art of leadership. Look for opportunities to lead. Coach an extracurricular activity or sports team. Volunteer to lead a fundraiser. Get involved in a local charitable foundation and take a leadership role. Teach a Sunday school class at your church. Join the PTO or school board.
- Expand your Theoretical Experiences by studying the science of leadership. For example, read a book about a great leader. Identify their "period of apprenticeship" and "rite of passage".
- Designate somewhere your Reflection Place. If you have a place to reflect, you will reflect. Make it a habit to go there and reflect on your leadership journey.

Experience is a great,
although sometimes hard, teacher.
—John Wooden

Chapter 3

PREPARATION NEEDS COMMITMENT

For most of my life I have believed that success is found in the running of the race. How you run the race—your planning, preparation, practice, and performance counts for everything. Winning and losing is a by-product, an aftereffect of the effort.

—Coach John Wooden

SUCCESS DOESN'T JUST HAPPEN. Success needs a strong and dedicated focus on preparation. However, preparation needs commitment and commitment takes extraordinary effort. Legendary coach John Wooden, who won ten NCAA basketball championships at UCLA, taught his basketball players that success is found in the running of the race and stressed that the big P, Process, drives each of the four small p's: planning, preparation, practice, and performance. Coach Wooden's relentless focus on the process rather than the outcome, produced extraordinary results.

It is the leader's responsibility to make sure team members are also prepared for each challenge. Effective leaders must set preparation expectations for team members. However, a strong and dedicated focus on preparation alone is not enough. Leaders need team members to commit themselves willingly to a desired level of preparedness. But remember, commitment is not free. Commitment takes extraordinary effort and it is the actions of the leader that drive discretionary effort.

Plain and simple, it is the leader's ability to influence individual behavior that determines the individual's level of commitment and, ultimately, their effort. It is the leader's responsibility to not allow team member's individual goals and set-backs to drive them away from team goals. In fact, this may be the toughest and also the most important aspect of leadership: the process of influencing human behavior to accomplish team or organizational goals.

Commitment Takes Extraordinary Effort

Effective leaders strive to find and maintain a balance between the needs and goals of the organization and the needs and goals of the people who make up the organization. The effective leader continually evaluates each team member's commitment, measured by their morale, esprit, discipline, and capability. These are the factors that influence individual effort. They are obviously important because effort produces results. However, effort is not fixed. It is discretionary.

Joe Torre played and managed in over 4,000 big league baseball games before he ever got to a world series. All that experience without a championship helped prepare him as manager of the New York Yankees. At the end of the 1995 season, when he accepted the position, many people thought he was crazy to work for notorious Yankee owner, George Steinbrenner. Torre, on the other hand, looked at it as an opportunity. He knew that Steinbrenner was a guy who would give him the tools to win. Then it would be up to him to prepare and lead the team to victory. He was not afraid of that challenge.

Joe Torre believed that competing on the highest level is not about winning. He thought winning was much more about preparation, courage, heart, and understanding and nurturing your people. He also believed that if his teams did all these things well, winning would be the result. He said, "Still, even with all the talent and resources we have here, having heart is what really makes the difference." Joe Torre wrote that for Business Week magazine in 2006, while still managing the

Yankees. Joe Torre understood that preparation needs commitment and commitment takes a lot of effort. He also appreciated the leadership challenge of nurturing commitment and effort.

In his book *The 21 Irrefutable Laws of Leadership*, John Maxwell introduces the Law of Connection. He writes, "To lead yourself, use your head; to lead others, use your heart." He also explains, "You can't move people into action unless you first move them with emotion. The heart comes before the hand." The Law of Connection emphasizes the importance of communication in order to pull commitment and effort from your team. It is the responsibility of the leader to find ways to pull the effort from team members required to develop team commitment. Joe Torre used the Law of Connection to pull commitment from his players, not to push it into them.

Preparation of the 1998 New York Yankees

Joe Torres' 1998 New York Yankee team was loaded with talent and is widely regarded as the one of the greatest all-time baseball teams. Torre's 1998 team was his most successful team. They won an American league record 114 regular season games. During the playoffs, they easily defeated the Texas

Rangers and Cleveland Indians to win the American League pennant. In the World Series, they swept the San Diego Padres, and Torre was voted Manager of the Year. In a late August interview, during the 1998 season, Torre was asked what made this team so different, and what was the key to their collective success so far into the year? He explained that the Yankees were focused completely on preparing themselves for each game they played, and that they went into each game with a renewed mindset to win.

The Steal

To emphasize the importance of preparation, Torre reminded his players of the 2004 American League Championship series (ALCS) against the Boston Red Sox. The Yankees had a commanding series lead: 3 games to 0. No team had ever come back from three games down to win the ALCS, and coming off a devastating 19–8 game three loss, things looked very bleak for the Red Sox.

In game four, at just past midnight in Fenway Park, Boston came to bat in the bottom of the ninth down a run, 4–3. The great Yankee closer, Mariano Rivera was on the mound. Rivera had a postseason record of 8–1 and .069 earned run average. Kevin Millar drew a lead-off walk, putting the tying run on first base. Then something unexpected happened.

Boston manager, Terry Francona, pinch ran Dave Roberts. Pinch running is not unusual in the situation; however, Roberts had not played in ten days. He spent most of the 2004 season with the Los Angeles Dodgers. The Red Sox picked him up at the trade deadline for just this situation. Despite his lack of playing time, Francona was not deterred from putting him in a position to turn the series around. Roberts stretched out and took his place on first base. Everyone knew what he was going to do.

To keep Roberts close to the bag, Rivera threw over to first base three consecutive times. On the first pitch to home plate, Roberts took off for second base. If he was unsuccessful, the Yankees would almost certainly have won the ALCS. But Roberts was safe. What followed became legendary. The next batter, Bill Mueller, singled and Roberts scored the tying run. The Red Sox won the game in 12 innings on a two-run walk-off homerun by David Ortiz! The Red Sox went on to win eight straight games to win the World Series. Their 2004 World Series Championship ended a run of 86 years between championships since their 1918 win.

Success is a testament to preparation.

Who would have guessed that little-known Dave Roberts would steal the most significant base in major league history?

Dave Roberts stole 243 bases during his 10 years in the major leagues. In his career, he stole only two postseason bases. The first of these two would spark a ninth inning rally that lead to eight straight wins and a curse-breaking World Series Championship. He was called upon to do a job he had prepared for each day his entire career. His success is a testament to preparation.

The Commitment of the 1992 Army Football Team

On 5 December 1992, at Veteran's Stadium in Philadelphia, the Army football team defeated Navy 25-24. It was the greatest comeback in the 93-year history of the Army vs. Navy football rivalry. But the story of this team actually begins one year earlier, on 6 December 1991, after Army's loss to a 0–10 Navy team. That night after the game, Coach Bob Sutton made a vow to himself that neither he nor his team would have that same feeling next year. The character and commitment of the 1992 Army team took shape that night in Philadelphia.

Prior to the team's first game, Coach Sutton outlined the 1992 season as the Take It Back Campaign. This season-long campaign consisted of four initiatives: Operation Jump Start (September), Operation Raging Fury (October), Operation

Relentless Rage (November), and Operation Desperation (December's Army vs. Navy game).

Take it Back Campaign

The seeds of Army's 1992 victory were sown back in February, when the whistle blew at 0500 hours on a Friday morning for the first of what Sutton called the "Dirty Dozen," predawn workouts to forge an attitude of total commitment and hard work.

The upperclassmen returned early in the summer. They bonded and defined effort and attitude expectations for the underclassmen, who later joined the team for their grueling workouts. These intense workouts created a sense of commitment, perseverance, and belief that would become the team's hallmark of the coming season.

Operation Jump Start

On 9 September, the Army football team stepped on the turf at West Point's Michie Stadium to confront their first opponent, Holy Cross. It had been seven months since the team first came together in February. The Holy Cross Crusaders were coming off an 11–0 season and 20-game winning streak, then the longest in collegiate football. Both teams started young, inexperienced quarterbacks. 19-year old Army quarterback, Mike Makovec, added a passing threat, something Army lacked in recent years with their wishbone offense. Despite it was his first varsity game, Makovec played well. He was 5 of 9 passing for 58 yards and no interceptions. He ran the wishbone well, gaining 47 yards on 18 carries. Seven of those yards were on a sprint to the end zone in the second quarter. Army held the lead at halftime 7–0.

Holy Cross managed a touchdown in the second half, but Army went on to win 17–7. After the game, Makovec said, "I was nervous all week long and throughout the game. When it was over, and I looked up at the scoreboard and saw we had won, that's when I finally relaxed." Although Army's offense fumbled the ball seven times, their defense rose to the occasion, stopping Crusader scoring on key drives and also blocking a punt. The Army team was now battle-tested. They had overcome adversity and were ready for their next challenge.

Following this win, the Army team headed south to Chapel Hill, North Carolina, to play the nationally ranked and already 2–0 Tar Heels. The spirited Army team did not back down. The score remained scoreless until midway through the second quarter when, oddly enough, a thunderstorm sent both teams to the locker room. The delay played in North Carolina's favor as they seized the momentum with two quick scores. The half ended with Army trailing 14–0. Army's defense settled down at half and the third quarter was a defensive battle, with neither team scoring. In the fourth quarter, Army pulled to within five points. But North Carolina scored late in the game to seal a 22–9 victory.

The game was a moral victory for Army, showing it could compete against a ranked team. However, the moral victory was bitter-sweet. Army lost quarterback, Mike Makovec to a knee injury. Sutton turned to 5-foot,10 inches, 175-pound sophomore Rick Roper to lead the offense. At the beginning of spring training, Roper was at the bottom of the depth chart. Now he found himself preparing to start the next game against The Citadel Bulldogs. Victorious over Army the year before, they came to Michie Stadium 3-0 with a No. 8 ranking in Division I-AA coaches' poll. The Bulldogs converted a late fourth quarter field goal to defeat Army, 15–14. It was not what the Bulldogs did in the game that made the difference; it was the lack of execution by Army, who failed to convert two of their own field goal opportunities. Senior kicker, Patmon Malcolm had a 53-yard attempt blocked and missed a 41-yard attempt.

Operation Jump Start ended with a disappointing 1–2 record. The Army team that had played so well against Holy Cross had not only lost two tough games, but also lost their starting quarterback in the process. With their backs against the wall and struggling with adversity, the Army team had a week off to prepare for their next challenge against Lafayette. This game marked the end of Operation Jump Start and the beginning of Operation Raging Fury.

Operation Raging Fury

Army's Homecoming brought the Lafayette Leopards to Michie Stadium. Unfortunately, the Leopards traveled to West Point without their star running back, Erik Marsh, who missed the weekend with the flu. Even so, the Leopards nearly defeated Army. With one minute remaining in the game and trailing by one point, Army took possession of the ball. They drove the field 57-yards to the Leopard's 26 yard line. In the drive, Roper completed passes of 13, 18, and 11 yards to set-up a winning field goal. With only 10 seconds on the clock, Malcolm converted the kick, and the Homecoming crowd went wild. As the team looked forward to their next two road games, Coach Sutton felt like Operation Raging Fury was off to a good start.

The Army team could not maintain the momentum. After a lop-sided loss to Rutgers (45–10) at Giants Stadium and a disappointing loss to bowl-bound Wake Forest (23–7) in Winston-Salem, the Army football team returned home to lick their wounds. At the midway point of the season, with a losing 2–4 record and no chance for a bowl game, most teams might have thrown in the towel. However, Coach Sutton rallied his team and challenged them to make "The Stand" for the remainder of the season.

To begin the second half of the season, the Army team welcomed the Eastern Michigan Eagles to West Point. The Eagles turned out to be the perfect tonic for a struggling Army football team. Army won the game 57–17. They dominated on both sides of the football, rushing for a season-high 450 yards while holding the Eagles to less than 100 yards rushing. Operation Raging Fury ended with a 2–2 record. Now the Army team readied themselves for Operation Relentless Rage. All three games in Operation Relentless Rage were played at home.

Operation Relentless Rage

The opening game of this campaign was a classic service academy battle against the Air Force Academy. After a 25–0 loss to Air Force in Colorado Springs the year before, Army was out for revenge on their home field.

Before a sellout crowd, the game turned into a defensive showdown and remained 0–0 into the 4th quarter. Air Force struck first with a 3-yard touchdown. The Army team could only manage a late field goal and lost 7–3. This was a devastating defeat that would clearly test the team's character going into the next game against Northern Illinois.

The Northern Illinois Huskies featured Division I-A third leading rusher, LeShon Johnson, who eventually finished sixth in the 1993 Heisman Trophy voting and was a third-round pick by the Green Bay Packers in the 1994 NFL draft. Johnson came into the game averaging nearly 133 yards per game. Coach Sutton called him "the best back we've ever played here." The Cadets rose to the occasion and defeated the Huskies, 21–14. The Huskies drew first blood, but the Cadets struck right back in the 1st quarter to tie the score and they never looked back. The Army team showed their character and responded by holding the nation's third leading rusher to just 68 yards, made three interceptions, and had two sacks. This victory gave the Army team momentum and set-up the final game of Operation Relentless Rage against the 19th ranked Boston College Eagles.

As 16-point underdogs, the Army Black Knights dug in and fought the Eagles valiantly. Army kept the game close and late in the fourth quarter scored a touchdown to make it 35–24. The game ended 41–24, Eagles, but it was much closer than the final score. In spite of their loss, the Army displayed tremendous effort and character on the field that day.

While a record of 4–6 is a losing record, the Army football team's character had been galvanized. The team now turned its focus to the single most important game of their season—The Army vs. Navy game.

Operation Desperation: The Army vs. Navy Game

One year earlier, as a freshman, Army's starting quarterback, Rick Roper, was so far down the depth chart, he didn't even make the road trips with the team. He didn't even have his name in the game program. Now, because of quarterback Mike Makovec's injury, he had been moved up to starting quarterback for the Army.

As the team left for Philadelphia, the Corps of Cadets and the West Point community provided a memorable sendoff. The Army team was determined to erase last season's nightmare 24–3 loss to a winless Navy team. As Coach Sutton's Army team entered Veteran's stadium, the final challenge in their Take It Back Campaign now stood before them.

Early in the game, the outcome for Coach Sutton and his Army team did not look good. Navy had delivered the first blow, and Army was down on the mat. It was at this moment, with a 4-6 record and trailing 17–0 in the second quarter, Sutton's Army team had all the reasons in the world to quit. At this point in the game, there was no reason to believe that this team could come back from trailing 17 points. However, it was Army's quarterback Rick Roper that led the charge. After a Navy score, Roper began a crucial drive and rallied his men with a 43-yard bootleg run around left end that set-up an eventual 2-yard touchdown run by Chad Davis. The first half ended, 17–7.

At the start of the second half, Army was forced to punt and Navy drove down the field to score a touchdown. The Navy team had fought back and, once again, Army found themselves down 17 points. Once again, there was no reason to think that the Army team could respond from 17 points down a second time. It looked all but over for Sutton's Army team.

Late in the third quarter, trailing 24–7, and facing adversity, Army's true character started to shine through. On a pivotal play, Army's Dan Davis sacked Navy's quarterback, causing a fumble that was picked up by Gary Graves and returned 22 yards to the Navy 22 yard line. On the next play, Roper ran a bootleg right for a touchdown, cutting the score to 24–14. Going into the final quarter, the momentum was shifting.

Army struck first in the fourth quarter. Roper connected on a 35-yard pass that set up a 68-yard touchdown pass to Gaylord Greene, the longest touchdown pass in the history of the rivalry. This cut the score to 24–20. But instead of kicking the extra point conversion, Coach Sutton called a fake. The holder, Chris Shaw, faked the hold and ran a bootleg around the right end for the 2-point conversion. With 7:23 left in the game, Army now trailed only 22–24.

Following an exchange of punts, Army was unable to move the ball and punted from their 43-yard line. Army's kicker and punter, Patmon Malcom, pinned the punt inside the one-yard line. Army's defense held Navy to a three and out, forcing Navy to punt out of their own end zone. With 2:15 left to play, Army took over on the 35-yard line but failed to convert a first down. On 4th down and 7 yards to go, there was only one option: to attempt a game-winning field goal.

The ball was marked on the 27-yard line, making it a 44–yard attempt. Malcom lined up and drilled it straight through the uprights. Michie Stadium erupted with celebration! But wait, there was a flag on the play. Army was penalized for delay of game, moving the ball back five yards for a 49-yard field goal. Malcom had to do the near impossible: kick the winning field goal a second time, and at an even tougher distance! Malcom steadied himself and kicked the ball perfectly straight through the uprights, capping one of the greatest comebacks in Army vs. Navy history!

In the locker room after the game, the Chief of Staff, four-star General Gordon Sullivan, congratulated the cadets saying, "You won a great win. The whole United States of America knows about it. Army beat Navy. That is a big deal. Character did it. Character did it. We're all proud of you…coaches… players…supporters. We're proud of you. That's what made America great. Sucking it up and winning." In the heat of the battle and the chaos of victory celebration, General Sullivan was able to see character at work and acknowledge it to the victors.

Along with character, the team's preparation and commitment were also summed up by Sutton's comments soon after the game, "There were a lot of big plays packed into the last quarter-and-a-half, but we didn't win it in the last 19 minutes. We won it throughout the season, overcoming adversity. You can't all of a sudden press a button and beckon that sort of resolve." It is motivation that drives discretionary effort. Sustained commitment benefits everyone!

Sustained commitment benefits everyone.

Joe Torre and Bob Sutton are tremendous leaders, who passionately believed that effective leadership takes planning and preparation. The courage of their conviction and relentless focus on the process rather than the outcome produced extraordinary results. These lessons help confirm that in order to achieve results, it takes strong and dedicated focus on preparation. It takes leadership to ignite the motivation required to sustain commitment. Continually motivating teams day in and day out is challenging work!

Motivation

Motivation is the "wanting" aspect of human behavior. In his seminal 1968 article "One More Time: How Do You Motivate Employees?" Frederick Herzberg wrote, "I can change a person's battery, and then recharge it, and recharge it again. But it is only when one has a generator of one's own that we can talk about motivation. One that needs no outside stimulation. One wants to do it." Herzberg describes the important difference between simple movement and real motivation. He uses a battery to illustrate this difference. Leaders can charge a person's battery, and continue to recharge it; however, true motivation

The combination of ability and motivation defines individual performance.

occurs only when someone has a generator of their own. Understanding this subtle difference is critical for all leaders. Herzberg's article is still very applicable today. I keep it handy and reread it from time to time, as I struggle with the challenges of motivation.

Individuals join organizations in order to satisfy certain needs. Accordingly, within an organization, each individual, by having joined that organization, is usually willing to accomplish a portion of the organizational goals without too much influence on the part of anyone, including their leader. The degree to which each individual is willing to do so varies according to a combination of their innate and learned ability and their motivation to do the task. This combination of ability and motivation defines individual performance, as shown in the Performance Equation:

$$\text{Performance} = \text{Capability} \times \text{Motivation}$$

Generally, an individual's ability is relatively easy to define, identify, and, in most cases, do something about, provided we select people who already have certain abilities or can be trained to do certain jobs. Motivation, on the other hand, is more difficult to grasp.

The word motivation comes from the Latin word "to move." Accordingly, motivation implies something that "energizes" action. However, in organizations, leaders are not only interested in energizing subordinates, but also providing "direction" to their energy. Furthermore, we want subordinates to continue to be energized in the proper direction, even when the leader is absent. This motivation is made up of three essential elements: energy, direction, and persistence. The Motivation Equation looks like this:

Motivation = Energy + Direction + Persistence

It is the leader's responsibility to provide the ingredients necessary for motivation. When our team members are motivated to do the job even when we are not around to lead them, then we've succeeded. This is what makes motivation critical and also difficult. It directly impacts the performance of each individual and in turn, the aggregate of each individual's performance determines the team's performance.

Chapter Three Summary

Preparation Needs Commitment

Preparation Need Commitment

- Preparation requires expectations.
- Leaders cannot allow the team member's individual goals or set-backs to drive them away from team goals.
- From author John Maxwell, "The heart comes before the head." You can't motivate action without first tapping into emotion.

Commitment Takes Effort

- A dedicated focus on preparation drives commitment.
- Commitment is not free—the leader's actions drive discretionary effort.
- It takes leadership to ignite the motivation required to sustain commitment.

The Performance Equation:

Performance = Capability x Motivation

- This combination of ability and motivation defines individual performance.

The Motivation Equation:

Motivation = Energy + Direction + Persistence

- Motivation drives discretionary effort.
- When our team members are motivated to do the job even when we are not around to lead them, then we've succeeded.

You can't move people to action
unless you first move them with emotion.
The heart comes before the head.
Therefore, effective leaders know that
you first have to touch people's hearts
before you ask them for a hand.
—John Maxwell

The credit belongs
to the man
who is actually
in the arena.

—Theodore Roosevelt

Appendix 1

Three Strategies to Start Your Leadership Journey

1. *Start your journey:* Look into the Twin Cities Leadership Academy's leadership coaching program. Email King@InPursuitofLeadership.com to learn more.

2. *Share the book:* Read this book in a management group or book club. Use the chapter exercises to apply the leadership principles you learn.

3. *Start or upgrade your apprenticeship experience:* Identify a leadership mentor, make contact, and start to build a relationship.

Effective leaders affect change, but you don't have to do it alone. Get the coaching and mentoring you need to successfully lead your team to higher performance.

For questions about these strategies,
email King@InPursuitofLeadership.com

Appendix 2

Cadet Prayer

O GOD, OUR FATHER,
Thou Searcher of human hearts,
help us to draw near to Thee
in sincerity and truth.

May our religion be filled with gladness and
may our worship of Thee be natural.

Strengthen and increase our admiration
for honest dealing and clean thinking, and
suffer not our hatred of hypocrisy and pretence
ever to diminish.

Encourage us in our endeavor to live above
the common level of life.

Make us to choose the harder right
instead of the easier wrong, and
never to be content with a half truth
when the whole can be won.

Endow us with courage that is
born of loyalty to all that is noble and worthy,
that scorns to compromise with vice and injustice and
knows no fear when truth and right are in jeopardy.

Guard us against flippancy and irreverence
in the sacred things of life.
Grant us new ties of friendship and
new opportunities of service.

Kindle our hearts in fellowship
with those of a cheerful countenance, and
soften our hearts with sympathy
for those who sorrow and suffer.

Help us to maintain the honor of the Corps
untarnished and unsullied, and
to show forth in our lives the ideals of West Point
in doing our duty to Thee and to our Country.

All of which we ask in the name of
the Great Friend and Master of all. AMEN.

—Clayton E. Wheat

Appendix 3

Recommended Leadership Books

Here is my list of the top 12 books on leadership. To strengthen your Leadership Formula, read one a month for one year.

1. *The 21 Irrefutable laws of Leadership* (Maxwell)
2. *Be, Know, Do: Leadership the Army Way* (Hesselbein & Shinseki)
3. *Plain Talk: Lessons from a Business Maverick* (Iverson)
4. *Leadership Is an Art* (De Pree)
5. *The West Point Way of Leadership* (Donnithorne)
6. *Duty Honor Country: West Point Fundamentals for Business Success* (Dorland & Dorland)
7. *Beyond Winning: The Timeless Wisdom of Great Philosopher Coaches* (Walton)
8. *The Essential Wooden: A Lifetime of Lessons on Leaders and Leadership* (Wooden & Jamison)
9. *Wooden on Leadership* (Wooden & Jamison)
10. *Robert E. Lee on Leadership* (Crocker)
11. *Coaching for Commitment: Interpersonal Skills for Obtaining Superior Performance* (Kinlaw)
12. *Leadership Challenge* (Kouzes & Posner)

About the Author

WILLIAM TYLER KING has been teaching at the University of Minnesota's Manufacturing Operations Management degree program since 2002 and served as the program's Faculty Director from 2006 to 2011. He received a B.S. in engineering in 1984 from the United States Military Academy at West Point. He attended the Defense Language Institute at the Presidio of Monterey, studied Dutch, and served in the U.S. Army as a liaison officer for NATO in Europe. He also served in the U.S. Army Reserves as a Company Commander in the 91st Training Division located in Fort Ord, California. In 2000, King obtained his M.S. in operations and technology management from Illinois Institute of Technology in Chicago. Since 2000, he has worked in the Chicago and Twin Cities areas in various operations leadership positions. He is CEO of King Business Consulting, Inc. and Founder of the Twin Cities Leadership Academy.